How To Use This

READ TOGETHER · DO TOGETHER

This is a very special book. Why? Because it's all about YOU!

Since it's your story, you can write or draw in the empty white boxes in the book. (A grown-up can help if you want.)

And don't worry if something doesn't turn out quite perfectly... that's what makes it special!

Read, draw, talk, laugh and have fun!

Georgia is home—and I think quite a lot
that I'm lucky to live in this wonderful spot.
Why is it special? That's easy to see.
It's the place that begins the whole story of me!

A picture of me

by Jashen

You

Age 7

Georgia roots keep me strong and it's really quite **neat** that the place they begin is my very own street.

Where I live

Buckea

It's close to

my aunt

Georgia is in the southeast part of the United States.

Southern charm is quite **famous** as everyone knows and the way that I speak is one way that it shows.

My Southern charm is hard to beat!

Yes Ma'am   Please   No Sir

How interesting! The state butterfly of Georgia is the Eastern Tiger Swallowtail.

Finding pals is not hard when you share common ground.
Sometimes friends are quite close if you just **look around**.

Good Friends!

is my favorite thing to do.

Georgia **cooks** are so skilled they can please any guest.
(No surprise that they think homemade food is the **best**.)

Fresh Peach Pie

Vidalia® Onion Relish

I love to eat

taco .

I didn't think I would like

pizza

...but I do!

The sweet Vidalia® onion
is only grown in Georgia.

Taking trips to the **park** makes me want to see more.
I have quite a long list of fun things to **explore**.

Georgia Trip List

- Stone Mountain Park
- Georgia Aquarium
- Jekyll Island

It was
fun to visit

my friend house.

Next up:

My grandparents

Can't wait to start packing!

In this state we make **noise** for our favorite home teams.
Win or lose—all great plays deserve very loud **screams**.

SCORE! **YAY!**

Go ahead! Color the T-shirt in your team colors!

Georgia land provides homes for more **critters** than me.
So it's good to **protect** even what we can't see.

please Don't Pollute!

Some of my favorite animals:

Many people from here have done things that are **great**.
Makes me **proud** to say I'm from the very same state.

MARTIN LUTHER KING, JR.
(Civil Rights Leader ~ Atlanta)

JULIETTE GORDON LOW
(Founder of Girl Scouts ~ Savannah)

JAMES E. CARTER, JR.
(39th U.S. President ~ Plains)

JULIA ROBERTS
(Actress ~ Smyrna)

GEORGIA BORN

CONGRATULATIONS TO MY HERO

I think

is great because

And guess what? You don't have to be famous to be a hero!

In Georgia good **music** will send out a beat
that will start in your ears but end up in your **feet!**

Songs I like to sing:

Talor Swiet

i

v

Ray Charles (Albany, GA) had a #1 hit when he sang the song "Georgia on My Mind."

Georgia people take pride in the things they **create**.
Bright ideas **shine** through from all over the state.

I'm pretty
good at making

pasta

and desserts.

In this state **celebrations** are always great fun.
People **laughing** and sharing is just how it's done.

Georgia became a state on January 2, 1788.

My favorite

celebration is

me

because

am a kid .

As my own **story** grows I will never forget
all the places I've been and the **people** I've met.
Yes, the **memories** I have of this wonderful place
are the ones that will always bring **smiles** to my face.

When I grow up I'd like to

be a cleaner

Keep exploring! Keep learning! Keep growing!

My Family Tree

Ashuan   Dad

mon   Jashua   A
        Me

grndm   S

urand f   A

f   m

Georgia Roots!

A tracing of my hand

My Time Capsule

Things you need:

- a cardboard box (big enough to fit this book and some other small things)
- one blank piece of paper and an envelope
- three index cards
- some favorite little "stuff" (like pictures, artwork, something that shows your favorite team on it)
- a recent newspaper
- tape and some ribbon

First: Fill out two of the index cards. On one, describe your perfect day. On the other, list the price of some things you often use or do.

My perfect day is when...

Milk costs
_____

A Movie ticket costs
_____

Next: Use the blank piece of paper to write a letter to your future self! When you are done, put it in the envelope and seal it shut.

Dear Future Me,
When I think about you in the future
I wonder...

Then: Put the index cards, this book, the letter to your future self and the other special "stuff" in the box. Wrap it like a present with the newspaper. Put ribbon around it. Then write on the last index card: DO NOT OPEN FOR 10 YEARS! and tape it to the box.

Finally: Put the box in the back of a closet or somewhere where you won't see it too much. Then wait ten years... and OPEN!

The countdown is starting!